My New Mommy

Written by Lilly Mossiano

Illustrated by Sage Mossiano

Published by Spun Silver Productions
spunsilverproductions.com
ISBN: 1482757192
ISBN-13: 978-1482757194

This is the first book in a series designed to aid in the fostering of acceptance and understanding of transgender individuals, more specifically in children who may or do have a trans* person in their life. This is its second release in print format. The second book, My New Daddy, published in January 2013, dealt with female to male transition. This book explains, in simple terms, male to female transition. Though the retitling of a parent is something that is as private a decision as transition itself, the use of "Daddy" and "Mommy" here are more strictly to explain the mental acceptance of Violet, our little narrator, then to indicate the need for such a title change.

ACKNOWLEDGMENTS

To list all the names of those that have assisted with the making of this book, from conception on would create a whole new book. So for those who are not mentioned, you have not been forgotten. Your support has been tremendous.

In particularly….

Sage Mossiano: without my illustrator and partner, I would be lost.

Mom and Dad: without the both of you supporting me and being there for me through this process, I would not have made it this far.

Adrian Michael: without your assistance, I never would have made it this far.

Philip Tolliver: without your assistance, and your expertise, I never would have made my deadlines.

For those who struggle each and every day.

Hi, my name is Violet, and this is what my daddy used to look like.

He used to have a beard. Then, one day, he shaved it off.

He used to have short hair. Then, over time, he let it grow out.

Then one day my daddy took me to get my ears pierced, so I could wear pretty earrings.

While I was getting my ears pierced he got his ears pierced as well.

My daddy sat down with me and explained to me that nature made a mistake and he should have been born a girl like me.

After our talk, my daddy started wearing dresses, and skirts. He also started going by a new name, and I started calling him "Mommy".

Each and every day, my daddy started looking more and more like a mommy and less like a daddy.

After some time, my new mommy went to the see a doctor. She needed to have an operation to make her become a girl like me.

Now I am a lucky little girl because my daddy is my new mommy. She will always love me and I will always love her.

Being transgender in today's society can be challenging. Without a lot of education or tolerance being taught, gender nonconforming individuals often find themselves in uncomfortable and often dangerous situations.

Below are resources to aid transgender and other gender nonconforming individuals in their journey. Some are support groups, others are law groups and advocacy centers that can help with discrimination cases and hate crimes.

You are **not** alone.

Transgender Resources:

Susan's Place: http://www.susans.org

GLAAD: http://www.glaad.org/transgender

PFLAG: http:// www. pflag .org

Human Rights Campaign: http://www.hrc.org/issues/transgender

The Transgender Law Center: http://transgenderlawcenter.org/

Wipe Out Transphobia: http://wipeouttransphobia.com

Lilly Mossiano is the author of My New Mommy and My New Daddy. She is an LGBT advocate, and a geek at heart. She is a fan of horror and sci-fi genres. She is currently working on several young adult and older children's books in those categories, as well as expanding the "My New" Series to include siblings and other family members, as well as address the other parents in My New Mommy and My New Daddy.

She lives in North Carolina with her wife and partner, Sage Mossiano.
You can find her on the following sites:

Facebook: http://www.facebook.com/LillyMossiano
Website: http://lillymossiano.wordpress.com

Made in the USA
Middletown, DE
28 November 2016